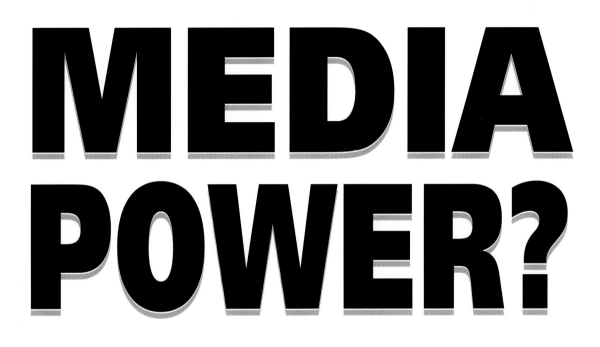

VIEWPOINTS

MEDIA POWER?

ALISON COOPER

SEA-TO-SEA
Mankato Collingwood London

This edition first published in 2006 by
Sea-to-Sea Publications
1980 Lookout Drive
North Mankato
Minnesota 56003

Printed in China

Library of Congress Cataloging-in-Publication Data

Cooper, Alison, 1967-
  Media power? / by Alison Cooper.
    p. cm. — (Viewpoints)
  Rev. ed. of: Media power? 1997
  Includes index.
  ISBN 1-932889-61-2
  1. Mass media—Juvenile literature. I. Title. II. Viewpoints (Sea to Sea Publications)

P91.2.C665 2005
302.23—dc22

                                        2004062522

9 8 7 6 5 4 3 2

Published by arrangement with the Watts Publishing Group Ltd, London

Picture acknowledgments:
The authors would like to thank the following
for permission to reproduce the photographs included in this book:
Cover photograph: Steve Shott. Corbis/Trapper Frank 8r;
Hulton/Deutsch Collection Ltd.: 14t, 14b; Larry White Agency, 13t;
Magnum Photos: Alex Webb 4, P. Jones-Griffiths 15b, 28t, Philip Ide, 22t;
PA Photos: William Conran 5t, Andrew Parsons 12; Panos Pictures/Mark
Henley 28b; Paul Lowe 7b, 11b, 27b, Steve Curry 17b; Martin
Parr/Magnum 25b; Rex Features Ltd.: 6b, 7t, 10t, 16, 17t, 18, 20, 23,
24t, 27t, 29t, 29b; Jonathan Banks 6t; David Hurrell 4t; Alex Woods 19t;
Mike Daines 8l, The Sun, 9b, Edwards/Miler, 10b. The Roland Grant
Archive: First Independent 9t, WB Prod. Ltd. 11t; Sipa Press: 15t, 21t,
21b, 22b, 26t; Cavalli, 8l; Sitting Images: David Constantine 4b;
Topham/Image Works 13t; Topham Picture Source 19b; Topham/Press
Association: 24b, 25t; Panos Pictures: Liba Taylor, 26b.

Quotation credits, given from the top of a page beginning with the left-
hand column.
pps 4/5 1 Media Ownership: The UK Government's Proposals,
Department of National Heritage, May 1995; 2 David Walsh, Selling Out
America's Children, 1994; 3 David Gauntlett, Moving Experiences:
Understanding Television's Effects and Influences, 1995; 4 Louis Heren,
The Power of the Press?, 1985; 5 UK Liberal Democrat policy paper, A
Free and Open Press, March 1995.
pps 6/7 1 Nanita Unnikrishnan and Shailaja Bajpai, The Impact of
Television Advertising on Children, 1996; 2 David Gauntlett, Moving
Experiences: Understanding Television's Effects and Influences, 1995 ; 3
David Walsh, Selling Out America's Children, 1994 ; 4 Radio Authority
Advertising and Sponsorship Code; 5 Larry Levite, president of
Algonquin Communications quoted in An Unfettered Press, U.S.
Information Service.
pps 8/9 1 Dee Dawson, who runs a clinic for anorexic children, quoted
in the Guardian, June 3, 1996; 2 Annie Morton, model, quoted in The
Guardian, June 3, 1996; 3 Alexandra Shulman, editor of Vogue, quoted
in the Observer, August 4, 1996; 4 British Board of Film Classification,
Annual Report 1994-5; 5 Trevor Phillips, TV presenter, quoted in The
Guardian, June 10, 1996.
pps 10/11 1 Dr. Park Deitz, chief psychiatrist of the FBI, quoted in The
Independent, April 30, 1996; 2 Dustin Hoffman, speech to Cannes Film
Festival on May 10, 1996 quoted in The Independent, May 11, 1996; 3
British Board of Film Classification press statement, December 1994; 4
Robert Yates in The Guardian, May 20, 1996; 5 BBFC Annual Report
1994-5.
pps 12-13 1 Lord Mackay, British Lord Chancellor quoted in The Times,
November 1995; 2 Judge Sanders, UK trial judge, quoted in The Times,
October 1995; 3 Judge Willem Van Schendel, No Silence in Court, 1995;
4 Fred Graham, chief anchorman of Court TV, quoted in The Times,
October 1995; 5 Roger Graef, Crime, Justice, and the Media, 1995.
pps 14/15 1 Denis Mack Smith, Mussolini, 1981; 2 William L Shirer, The
Rise and Fall of the Third Reich, 1960; 3 Article 19, United Nations
Universal Declaration of Human Rights; 4 Robert S. Peck, Constitutional
Protection.
pps 16/17 1 Nicholas Coleridge, Paper Tigers, 1993; 2 Media Ownership:
The UK Government's Proposals, Department of National Heritage, May
1995; 3 Nicholas Coleridge, Paper Tigers, 1993; 4 Mauro Paissan,
Italian opposition politician with responsibility for state television, 1994;
5 The American Press, the Center
for Foreign Journalists.
pps 18/19 1 Andrew Marr, editor, The Independent, June 7, 1996; 2
Andrew Neill, former editor of The Sunday Times quoted in The
Guardian, July 21, 1996; 3 Daily Mirror, September 1992; 4 Gore Vidal,
author and political commentator.
pps 20/21 1 Chicago Tribune newspaper
January 1992; 2 David Warden, chairman,
McCann-Erickson advertising agency, quoted in The Independent; 3
U.S. Elections 96, U.S. Information Agency; 4 Ben Macintyre, The Times,
October 1999; 5 Andreas Whittam-Smith, The Independent, August 26,
1996.
pps 22/23 1 Henry Porter, Lies, Damned Lies, and Some Exclusives,
1984; 2 BBC guidelines for producers; 3 Leonard Dowie, executive
editor, Washington Post quoted in An Unfettered Press, U.S. Information
Service; 4 Charles Moore, editor, The Telegraph, quoted in The
Guardian, May 1996; 5 Rupert Murdoch, newspaper owner, quoted in
The Power of the Press?, 1985.
pps 24/25 1 The Sun newspaper, September 1992; 2 Andrew Marr,
editor of The Independent, June 7, 1996; 3 Paul Dacre, editor of the
Daily Mail newspaper, quoted in The Guardian, June 10, 1996; 4 Lord
Wakeham, Chairman, Press Complaints Commission, quoted in The Mail
on Sunday, 1995.
pps 26/27 1 John Simpson, a BBC foreign correspondent, quoted in The
Guardian, May 1, 1996; 2 Marshall McLuhan, The Montreal Gazette, May
16, 1975; 3 Philip Knightly, The First Casualty, 1975.
pps 28/29 1 and 2 Nanita Unnikrishnan and Shailaja Bajpai, The Impact
of Television Advertising on Children, 1996; 3 The Sun newspaper, May
22, 1996; 4 The Independent, June 25, 1996; Michael Kinsley, editor of
web magazine Slate, quoted in The Guardian, May 20, 1996.

Contents

Media power?

❝ The power of the media to influence and form opinion makes it an industry like no other. ❞
UK government proposals on media ownership

❝ A 30-second spot during the Super Bowl cost $900,000. Why did advertisers pay it? Because they knew it was worth the money. ❞ David Walsh, Selling Out America's Children

The "media" is a term for methods of mass communication such as movies, television, radio, newspapers, magazines, and the Internet. New technology is changing the media industry at a phenomenal rate. As it changes and expands, its potential to influence more and more areas of our lives raises many questions. What is the nature of its influence? Does it have a positive or negative effect on individuals and on society? Who controls it? Does it exercise its power responsibly?

Most people agree that what we see and hear via the media does produce a response in us. For example, watching a sad movie can make us cry, a television sitcom sometimes makes us laugh, and a disturbing news report can make us feel afraid or angry. Advertisers certainly believe that the media can have an effect on people; if they did not, there would be no reason for the advertising industry to exist.

Many people believe that if the words and images carried by the media can influence the way we spend our money, they must also influence other aspects of our behavior and the way we think.

▲ *In the modern world, there is no escape from the media. Advertising billboards in the street, newspapers, radio, television, and the Internet all bombard us with information.*

Other people feel that the issue is not that straightforward.

❝ [The effect of advertising] is radically different from the other alleged effects of television, such as the promotion of violence.... The choice between soap powders A and B can in no way be compared to the 'choice' of whether or not to go out and commit a violent act. ❞
David Gauntlett, Moving Experiences: Understanding Television's Effects and Influences

In some areas of society the media can be seen as a powerful force for good, as the Watergate affair in the early 1970s showed.

Two journalists working for the *Washington Post* uncovered corruption at the heart of the U.S. government, and their revelations led eventually to the collapse of President Nixon's administration. The right of the media to question the government can provide vital protection for freedom and democracy.

❝ Newspapers are the watchdogs of the public interest and the citizen's freedom is that much more secure as long as they continue to bark. ❞
Louis Heren, The Power of the Press?

In recent years, people have become more concerned about the way in which the media exercises its power.

Much of its output can seem trivial and sleazy. The motives of those who own and control it have been questioned. Such concerns have led to calls for governments to introduce stronger controls. Yet this too has proved controversial and difficult.

❝ ...those most in favor of muffling the press are often those who are seeking to keep from the public information which they have a right to know. ❞
UK Liberal Democrat Party policy paper

The challenge for the media is to find ways of using its power effectively, while striking a balance between its rights and its responsibilities.

Hard sell?

How much power does the advertising industry have? Billions of dollars are spent by advertisers in an attempt to persuade us that their product is better or trendier than those of their rivals. The question of how much impact their efforts have upon us is a controversial one.

66 Advertising creates false needs...products that are really needed require no advertising and therefore advertising promotes products that are not needed. 99
Nanita Unnikrishnan and Shailaja Bajpai, The Impact of Television Advertising on Children

▼ Supplying demand—or encouraging greed? Toy advertising on TV has been banned in some countries because of concerns about its effects on children.

▲ A right to choose? Companies offer fizzy bottled drinks that contain alcohol. These are meant for adults, but many parents complain that the product encourages children to drink alcohol.

By promoting products that are not needed, say the critics, advertising encourages greed and envy. It helps to create a wasteful society in which goods are thrown out long before they are worn out. Defenders of advertising say that ads are not that powerful. They do not create a need; they simply extend choice.

66 ...advertising is about shopping and shopping is something which most people do anyway. Advertising can make some products seem more attractive than others, even where they are substantially the same, and thus influences our purchasing decisions. 99 David Gauntlett, Moving Experiences: Understanding Television's Effects and Influences

Although there is concern about the effects of advertising in general, there is more concern about the effects of advertising on children and young people. Teenagers are especially vulnerable to brand advertising for products such as clothes, drinks, and computer games. Young people have a strong desire to conform, and wearing the right brand can give them a sense of security, reassuring them that they are "part of the group."

However, the pressure to buy specific brands can cause problems for many families.

"Nike, Starter, Reebok…[these] are household words, conjuring up images of speed, power, status, and perfection. For any parent trying to stick to a household budget, these words may also bring to mind arguments with children in a shoe store over a one-hundred dollar pair of sneakers."
David Walsh, Selling Out America's Children

Most countries have introduced rules to protect young people from being influenced by advertising in this way.

"Advertisements must not lead children to believe that unless they have or use the product advertised they will be inferior in some way to other children or liable to be held in contempt or ridicule."
Radio Authority, Advertising and Sponsorship Code

Even with these rules in place, however, pressure to look the same as friends and schoolmates continues to make strongly branded products objects of desire.

The issue of advertising power extends beyond its influence over the individual shopper. The media industry largely depends on advertising money to survive, so pleasing the advertisers can become as important as pleasing the public.

▲ Teenagers feel the pressure to dress in the latest fashions and "in" labels, spending a fortune on clothes that go swiftly out of date.

"Without the advertisers you are out of business; without the listeners you are out of business."
Larry Levite, president of Algonquin Communications

Advertisers look for ways to reach mass audiences or specific social groups. The media's efforts to meet the needs of advertisers can affect the type of programs that are made, the time at which they are shown, and the choice of stories that are featured in magazines or

▲ Sponsorship takes advertising off the newspaper page or TV screen, and into our everyday lives.

newspapers. With so much potential to influence so many aspects of our daily lives, it is vital that the industry exercises its power responsibly.

Hidden messages?

Advertisers set out to make an impression on us, yet the words and images of advertising make up only a small proportion of the "hidden messages" that we subconsciously receive every day. Over time, such messages can have a powerful impact on our attitudes toward ourselves and other people.

Images of thin, attractive, young women and good-looking, muscular men appear every day in magazines, the movies, and on television. There is concern that this can cause unhappiness and poor self-esteem among ordinary men and women, who feel that they look old, scrawny, or unattractive in comparison. Some people are worried that the importance given to body image is leading to health problems for the models and actors, and for those who strive to look like them. More young men are turning to drugs such as steroids to help build muscle strength, but many are unaware of the damaging side effects. Eating disorders such as anorexia can affect men as well as women, and surveys suggest that even young children are becoming worried about their weight.

66 *There is a problem for the 16- and 17-year-old girls who see…pictures [of very young, thin models] in magazines and will aspire to a figure that is completely impossible.* 99 *Dee Dawson, who runs a clinic for anorexic children*

But many people working in the industry believe that the critics are simply scaremongerers.
66 *It's going a bit far to suggest someone's anorexic just by looking at a picture…I can say that the business does not put pressure on me to keep my weight down.* 99 *Annie Morton, model*

▼ *Not the average boy next door; the muscular movie star Vin Diesel.*

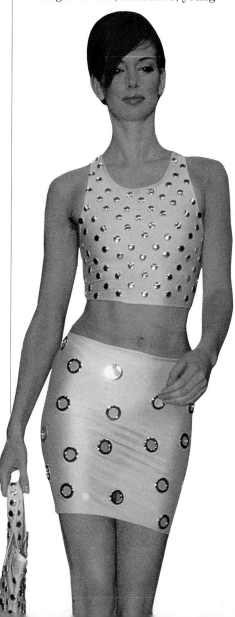

◄ *Do images of super thin models in fashion magazines make readers unhappy with their own body shape?*

Others argue that it is silly to suggest that magazines can have so much influence.

66 We have a way of reading and filtering this information.… No one looks at those magazines and thinks, 'I want to look like that.'.… No one is that stupid. 99 Alexandra Shulman, editor of British Vogue

The influence of the media on people's self-image causes concern, but there are areas in which its effects are considered even more damaging. Pornographic movies and magazines, for example, can reinforce negative attitudes toward women.

▶ *Some people argue that the media often portrays women as sex objects. Does this encourage sexist behavior in real life?*

66 American research…indicates that men who are predisposed to find rape enticing, or who find it hard to sympathize with victims of sexual assault, can have their prejudices reinforced by scenes in which women are forced…to respond to the sexual needs of others. 99 British Board of Film Classification, annual report

▲ *Can stereotypical images of black people in movies and on TV reinforce prejudice?*

The persistent use of stereotypical characters can affect attitudes toward whole groups in society.

66 Every imaginary young black thief or underachiever…makes life harder for real black people. When all that many white employees see of young black men is mugshots on crime shows, is it any wonder that three out of five black men in London are unemployed? 99 Trevor Phillips, politician and TV presenter

The question is, though, does the media distort attitudes and assumptions—or does it simply reflect the distortion and prejudice that are already present in society?

License to kill?

Can the messages people receive from the media affect not just their attitudes and the way they spend money, but also their behavior?

In 1999, two students at Columbine High School in Colorado shot and killed 12 other students and a teacher, before taking their own lives. They were reportedly influenced by a movie about a school shooting and by rock stars like Marilyn Manson. Media coverage led to other "copycat" attacks on schools.

" Presumably what happened was this man was sitting in Australia watching the emotional pictures from Dunblane and…he realized that Thomas Hamilton [the Scottish gunman] had a tremendous impact on the whole nation. " *Dr. Park Deitz, chief psychiatrist of the FBI*

Some are concerned that even fictional portrayals of violence can have a negative effect on people's behavior.

" Look at this global community we live in and what happens in Tasmania and what happens in Scotland. Are you saying [movie violence] doesn't have anything to do with it?… If kids are seeing violence in front of them…they are going to do the same thing. " *Dustin Hoffman, speech to Cannes Film Festival*

▲ *32 people died in Tasmania at the hands of one gunman. Was he driven by a desire to gain worldwide fame?*

◄ *The actor Dustin Hoffman has starred in violent movies in the past but now refuses to accept such roles.*

Following the release of the movie *Natural Born Killers* in 1994, it was claimed that several copycat killings had taken place in the USA and France. In the UK, there were many calls for the movie to be banned. Yet the British Board of Film Classification (BBFC) decided against such a ban, after investigating the cases involved.

▶ Natural Born Killers: *director Oliver Stone was sued by people who believed his movie had sparked copycat killings in the USA.*

❝ *The idea that ordinary people had been turned into killers by being exposed to a particular film was not one with which the FBI or local police forces in America had any sympathy.* ❞
BBFC press statement

Research into the wider issue of the link between screen violence and violence in society reveals that even violent offenders are no more likely to have seen controversial movies than their law-abiding peers, and such movies are rarely mentioned as favorite viewing. But for an increasing number of people the mere possibility that there could be a link makes increased censorship a sensible precaution. The video distribution company Warner Home Video was responding to this view when it postponed the video release of *Natural Born Killers* indefinitely.

However, greater use of censorship creates new problems. Banning a movie can actually increase people's desire to see it. If violent movies are removed from mainstream movie theaters, audience demand might be met by an unregulated "underground"

▶ Violence *has become a part of our society. Do moviemakers have a duty to reflect this—or does their work just make the problem worse?*

industry. People of different ages and social backgrounds have different ideas about acceptable viewing, so who decides what can be shown? Do those calling for increased censorship represent the majority view, or are they simply making the most noise?

❝ *It may be premature to start fretting about a U.S.-style 'moral majority' crusade across the arts, but…there, lobby groups have long realized that the most effective targets are the vast corporations which control the film distributor.* ❞
The Guardian newspaper

If violence is a part of society, can we blame moviemakers for depicting violence in their work?

❝ *It will be difficult for Hollywood to come to grips with the culture of violence in entertainment until America comes to grips with the culture of violence in society.* ❞
BBFC annual report

Trial by media?

When a crime takes place, it is a journalist's job to be first with the story—and to tell it better than anyone else. But questions are often asked about the lengths to which some journalists are prepared to go in pursuit of a story. There is concern that their behavior is having a damaging effect on the legal system and is even affecting people's

▼ British farmer Tony Martin shot and killed a 16-year-old burglar in 1999. After his release from prison in 2003, newspapers wanted to buy his story.

chances of getting a fair trial.

It has now become quite common for important witnesses in major trials to be "bought up" before the trial takes place. Large payments are promised in return for an exclusive story, to be published once the accused has been convicted. The problem is that if the accused person is not convicted, the stories are not of much interest. Many people are concerned that this encourages witnesses to exaggerate when they give evidence. Yet those who want

the practice to be banned may be oversimplifying the issue by blaming the media.

66 *...when a case [acquires] a certain degree of notoriety, people want to read about it, and that's what gives rise to the value of these contributions. It's easy to say it shouldn't happen, it's not so easy to see how you can prevent it happening and produce a better situation.* 99 *Lord Mackay, former British Lord Chancellor*

In Britain in 1995, a court case was dropped before trial for the first time because of concern that media coverage had made it impossible for a jury to reach a fair verdict. The defendant, Geoff Knights, had received so much press attention because of his relationship with a famous soap actress.

" *I have absolutely no doubt that the mass of media publicity in this case was unfair, outrageous, and oppressive.* **"**
Judge Sanders, trial judge

Journalists involved in crime coverage believe that such concerns are overstated. They argue that if juries are properly directed by the judge, they are quite capable of reaching a verdict on the basis of the evidence presented in court. Similar arguments over the role of the judge have been raised in relation to the televising of trials.

Some judges believe that cameras in court can have a negative effect on the way the trial is conducted, with witnesses being afraid to tell the truth, for example.

" *It is of vital importance that an atmosphere is created in the courtroom where everyone can speak freely.... Sound and picture clearly can interfere with the judicial process.* **"** *Judge Willem Van Schendel, No Silence in Court*

Supporters of cameras in court argue that televising cases helps the public to understand court procedures. They also say that it is the judge's responsibility to ensure that the cameras do not interfere with the court process.

" *The camera does not affect court process; that depends on the judge.* **"** *Fred Graham, chief anchorman, Court TV*

▲ *TV cameras have been allowed into U.S. courtrooms for many years. Would they help people in other countries understand how the courtroom works? Or would cameras simply glamorize the criminal process?*

Many people believe that the real problem with crime coverage is that there is simply too much of it.

" *The press...over-represents the level of violent crime in particular, and this has an important role in shaping popular views, including fear of crime.* **"** *Roger Graef, Crime, Justice and the Media*

Critics argue that the media can scare the public unnecessarily by making crime seem more of a problem than it really is, leading to calls for politicians to take tougher action against criminals. This may be no bad thing—but it highlights the extent to which the media can influence public and private opinion.

State control?

Media coverage can be very powerful. There is widespread agreement that when the state controls the media, censorship and propaganda can take the place of accurate information and can be used to very dangerous effect.

In the 1930s, fascist regimes led by Hitler in Germany and by Mussolini in Italy took control of the press and broadcasting. Through censorship and propaganda, Hitler and Mussolini aimed to make their people absolutely obedient,

▲ *Adolf Hitler's fascist regime used propaganda effectively to influence public opinion in Germany in the 1930s and 1940s.*

not just in their actions but even in the way they thought.

❝*By commanding all public means of communication, Mussolini [the Italian leader] could persuade public opinion that the outside world admired fascism as a new type of civilization.* ❞
Denis Mack Smith, Mussolini

◀ *Millions of people tuned in to radio bulletins during the Second World War. Censorship of the news was accepted as necessary.*

Once the regimes controlled public attitudes in their own countries they were able to pursue extreme policies, virtually without opposition. In Germany, such policies included programs to wipe out entire sectors of society, such as the Jewish and gypsy communities.

❝*No one who has not lived for years in a totalitarian land can possibly [imagine] how difficult it is to escape the dread consequences of a regime's calculated and incessant propaganda.* ❞ *William L. Shirer, The Rise and Fall of the Third Reich*

After the Second World War, the newly created United Nations took measures to protect the media from government interference in the future.

66 Everyone has the right to freedom of opinion and expression; this right includes freedom…to seek, receive, and impart information and ideas through any media. 99 Article 19, United Nations Universal Declaration of Human Rights

Many governments—especially in Communist and some developing countries—continued to exercise firm control over the media. Such systematic control is rarer today, but journalists who criticize their governments can face persecution.

Amnesty International receives reports from all over the world of journalists being imprisoned or attacked by state security services.

In Niger in 1998, for example, "antigovernment" radio stations were closed down and the journalists working there arrested. In China, one journalist was imprisoned for 11 years for sending e-mails abroad; another was imprisoned for making contact with foreign journalists.

State control of television is widespread, with the movements of foreign journalists often restricted. The flow of information on the Internet, however, is difficult to control.

Can state censorship and propaganda ever be justified? Many people believe that it is in wartime—when information could give an advantage to the enemy or result in loss of life. But even in this situation, there is a danger that censorship can cover up military incompetence and propaganda can be used to ensure continued public support for those in power.

▲ Political protests and human rights abuses in countries such as Myanmar (Burma) often go unreported because of government restrictions on foreign journalists.

However, those who are opposed to state censorship are aware that uncontrolled freedom of expression can have its drawbacks.

66 …when interests clash, as they often do, when the message is hateful, or hurtful or embarrassing, when one person's freedom of expression begins to affect the rights of others, it becomes a most difficult right to adjudicate. 99 Robert S. Peck, Constitutional Protection

◀ Should Ku Klux Klan members have the right to express racist views in the media?

Media moguls?

The media industry today is multinational and is worth billions of dollars. A relatively small number of people control the media. Rupert Murdoch, for example, owns nearly 200 newspapers, a movie studio, and several TV networks.

66 *The great new media empires spanning the world have [conquered] more territory in a decade than Alexander the Great or Genghis Khan in a lifetime.* 99 *Nicholas Coleridge, Paper Tigers*

As we have seen (pages 14-15), it is considered very dangerous for the state to control the media. Might not the growth of private media empires be equally dangerous?

66 *Free and diverse media are an indispensable part of the democratic process. They provide the [range] of voices…that inform the public, influence opinion, and [produce] political debate…. If one voice becomes too powerful, this process is placed in jeopardy and democracy is damaged.* 99 *British government proposals on media ownership, 1996*

▲ *As rules on media ownership are relaxed, Rupert Murdoch is poised to expand his global media empire.*

What happens if media owners use their power to try to turn public opinion against abortion rights, or against black people, or to promote their own brand of religion?

66 *…the notion that unsupervised private individuals can own newspapers is sinister and even repellent.* 99 *Paper Tigers*

The situation is potentially more dangerous if a media owner achieves political power. There was great concern in Italy in 1994 when Silvio Berlusconi, who owned 85 percent of commercial Italian television stations, was elected Prime Minister. Some politicians believed that his media power had played a part in his victory. After he was reelected in 2001, his government introduced a bill two years later to abolish restrictions on the cross-ownership of television stations and newspapers, but the Italian parliament blocked it by voting against the bill.

66 *…these advertisements…are made of propaganda in favor of the government and are of no help to the citizen at all.* 99 *Mauro Paissan, Italian opposition politician with responsibility for state television*

Another cause for concern is that media owners are business people who want to make money. This means producing programs and newspapers that appeal to large audiences and that attract many advertisers.

▲ Many Italians were concerned that Silvio Berlusconi's dominance of the media and politics was a threat to the country's political freedom.

66 *Competition for the advertising dollar is fierce. Critics say this contributes heavily to a policy of pandering to an audience's desires and prurient tastes.* 99
The American Press by the Center for Foreign Journalists

Governments have taken steps to protect people from the potential dangers of the privately owned media. They have introduced rules on who can own broadcasting stations, regulations about what can be broadcast, and limits on the number of media outlets an individual can own.

▶ Evangelists often use TV to spread their religious messages. There are dangers if one voice or one message becomes too dominant.

However, with the rapid development of the worldwide Internet and the many new channels offered by digital broadcasting, some people argue that it will be impossible for one voice to become dominant among so many.

But when American rules on media ownership were relaxed in 2003, many people warned that private monopolies would be created, making the freedom of the media little more than a comforting illusion.

In the public interest?

Under a repressive regime, the media can be in danger from the government. In a free and democratic society, can the government be in danger from the media?

66 *The right of journalists, like other citizens to ask questions, probe, and challenge is essential.... Sniffing out double standards and hypocrisy also means, on occasions, reporting the gap between what powerful people say and what they do in bed or behind closed doors.* 99 *Andrew Marr, former editor of the Independent newspaper*

Revelations about the private lives of

politicians can raise important questions about their honesty and make us ask whether they are fit to represent us. Sometimes the benefits of such revelations are debatable. Does the threat of media exposure mean that talented people with less-than-perfect private lives dare not stand for public office, or are the media doing a useful job?

66 *Fear of disclosure and of public disgrace is what keeps a lot of our politicians...on the reasonably straight and narrow.* 99 *Andrew Neill, former editor of the Sunday Times newspaper*

◀ Hillary Clinton's dignified response to her husband's affairs improved her media image and encouraged her to revive her political career.

In 2001, the author and British politician Jeffrey Archer was sentenced to four years in prison. He was found guilty of lying in court and perverting the course of justice in his 1987 libel suit against the *Daily Star*. The newspaper reported that Archer had slept with a prostitute. At the time many people felt he was the victim of a battle among the tabloids for increased sales. But Archer lied and used a false alibi and diary to clear his name. The tabloid press argued that they had been right to tell the voters what he was really like.

66 *Get caught out lying, cheating, freeloading, and nowadays you're the victim of a circulation war.* 99
Daily Mirror newspaper

Was the media acting in the interests of the voters? Compare the experience of President Clinton. Graphic details about his sexual relationship with a White House intern appeared in the media, and on the Internet as part of an official report, but his ratings in the opinion polls remained high and efforts to remove him from office failed. This might suggest that the voters are less concerned about the private

▲ *Some people thought Jeffrey Archer (center) had damaged the reputation of politics when he was found guilty of lying in court and sentenced to four years' imprisonment in 2001. He was released in 2003 after serving half his sentence.*

▼ *President Nixon could have used the help of today's imagemakers in his electoral battle with good-looking J.F. Kennedy.*

behavior of people in power than some of the media claim.

Personal image is another crucial factor in politics. Looking right for the job can be as important as having the best policies. Richard Nixon, the Republican candidate for the presidency in the 1959 elections, found himself at a disadvantage because he looked rather disreputable on television. The Democrats exploited this with the slogan "Would you buy a used car from this man?" Their candidate, John F. Kennedy, was helped by his movie-star good looks. In more recent times, Al Gore's 2000 campaign for the presidency was hampered by media emphasis on his "dull" character. In Britain, the same was said about the Conservative Prime Minister John Major.

❝ *To be perfect for television is all a President has to be these days.* ❞
Gore Vidal, author and political commentator

If this is true, it suggests that the media's influence on political life is not always in the public interest.

Substance—or soundbites?

66 *To no small extent, political attitudes and what might be called the public agenda are set by who appears on Nightline…Larry King Live, Crossfire, and other [TV] programs.* 99
Chicago Tribune newspaper

During an election campaign, most ordinary voters rely on the media for information about the important issues. Political parties have become skilled at managing the media, in order to display themselves, their products, and their policies in the best possible way. This is called "spin," but does it help people to make informed choices?

A favorite tactic used by political PR agents to make their own party look good is to make the "other side" look bad. Opposing parties often use press briefings or off-the-record conversations with friendly journalists to publicize mistakes the opposition has made. The hope is that a small problem or misjudgment can be hyped up by the media into a full-blown scandal.

66 *Negative campaigning works. It's easier and more effective to attack your opponents. Defending your own record, warts and all, is too vulnerable.* 99 *David Warden, former chairman, McCann-Erickson advertising agency*

Some people argue that this approach makes politicians more accountable for their mistakes.

▼ *Advertising can be used to create fear and distrust of the opposition among the public, as this UK Conservative poster attacking the Labour Party shows.*

However, others blame it for turning some media debates into mere mudslinging—where personalities, rather than issues, are attacked.

Politicians also rely heavily on advertising to get the message across, but television advertising in particular is very expensive. This raises an important issue in relation to election campaigns.

66 *With so many primaries scheduled for the same time, it would be impossible to campaign in all the states or even most of them. The only solution: use television advertising.... This means that the heavy advantage...goes to the candidate with the greatest war chest, that is, money to spend on his campaign.* 99 *U.S. Information Agency*

Should it be the candidate with the most money to spend who has the best chance of winning—or the candidate with the best policies?

Just before presidential campaign in 2000 several candidates were forced to drop out through lack of funds even before the preliminary voting rounds had taken place. This left party supporters with a much narrower choice.

66 *Candidates have been forced out by poverty in every American election but never so many, so early. Indeed the fundraising scramble has now replaced the primary process of winnowing out the presidential field. As she dropped out of the contest, Elizabeth Dole declared that 'Money is the bottom line.'* 99 *Ben Macintyre, The Times*

▲ Many election campaigns are fought using slogans such as the one on the side of this bus.

Some journalists would argue that the political parties themselves prevent voters from receiving more detailed information. Techniques such as issuing snappy soundbites, avoiding unpopular issues, and keeping controversial politicians out of the public eye, can all be used by

▼ Party conventions and conferences are no longer the place to discuss important issues; the aim is to put on a show for the voters watching at home.

"spin doctors" to keep their political message simple and attractive.

66 *The list of subjects not debated during a general election campaign can be extraordinary.... The party managers want to close down debate; the media must force it open.* 99 *Andreas Whittam-Smith, the Independent newspaper*

In the battle between the media and politicians, the media perhaps needs to develop new tactics to get at the substance behind the spin.

Telling it straight?

In the age of communications satellites and the Internet, more sources of information exist about events and issues at home and abroad than ever before. How does the media treat information? Are we well informed, or misinformed?

Only the biggest and most prestigious organizations can afford to keep many reporters "in the field." Most rely heavily on news agencies, press releases, and briefings from government sources, political parties, campaigning organizations, and businesses to provide them with information.

66 Much of the content of the national press is inspired by companies wishing to plug some product, some service, or some personality, and is therefore little more than covert advertising. 99
Henry Porter, Lies, Damned Lies, and Some Exclusives

The source of the information perhaps does not matter very much, as long as it is properly identified and treated in a balanced way. Most broadcasting organizations are legally required to do this, at least in their news coverage.

▼ Press conferences only give one side of the story. A journalist needs to check several sources to give a balanced point of view.

▲ Grabbing the headlines? Businessmen such as Britain's Richard Branson have become skilled in arranging eye-catching publicity opportunities to attract media coverage.

66 A reporter's opinion should not figure into the story at all. What a reporter contributes to a story is expertise and analysis. 99 Leonard Dowie, executive editor, Washington Post newspaper

Leading broadcasters in the UK also pride themselves on their impartial reporting.

66 The notion of impartiality lies at the heart of the BBC.... We must not recycle received opinion as though it were unassailable truth. We must be alert to the dangers of stereotypes and preconceptions... 99
BBC guidelines for producers

However, it can be very hard to report issues totally impartially. The prominence that is given to one story over another, and tiny differences in the use of language can imply support or criticism, so even when newspapers are careful they may still be attacked for biased reporting.

The British press does not even set out to offer an impartial view. The way in which news is reported can be influenced by various factors: the need to please the owner; to attract advertiser; or a wish to promote a particular political or social agenda.

66 *The Daily Telegraph is Tory… we advance a strongly conservative (and generally Conservative) political line in the paper.* **99** *Charles Moore, editor, the Telegraph newspaper*

Newspaper owners see nothing sinister in this—they are reflecting their readers' interests rather than influencing them.

66 *The public certainly has no duty to support newspapers. It is the duty of the publisher to provide the type of newspaper the public wants to read.* **99** *Rupert Murdoch, newspaper owner*

Many people would argue, however, that if a newspaper is tailored to the interests of its readers it can sometimes be difficult for the readers to gain an impression of what is really important. All the facts need to be known—and the facts need to be clearly separated out from opinion—to discover the whole truth behind any media story.

▼ *"Civil rights campaigners" or "rowdy lawbreakers"? Reporting of protests such as this can vary greatly between newspapers, with readers sometimes unaware of how they are being influenced by the choice of language.*

Invasion of privacy?

Politicians, pop stars, and princesses all attract a great deal of media attention as they carry out their roles. Most of them thrive on it, even using the attention to promote good causes, but when journalists ask questions about their private lives, they are usually less pleased to be in the spotlight. When does media interest become an unacceptable invasion of privacy?

For some journalists, especially those working for tabloid newspapers, the issue is a simple one.

66 The acid test of whether a story should be published is simple. Is it true? If it is, and the truth hurts, that is no argument for suppression. 99
The Sun newspaper

▲ *For ordinary people who find themselves in the news, facing the media circus can be a traumatic experience.*

▼ *Movie star Richard Gere and his supermodel wife Cindy Crawford tried to end media gossip about their marriage by putting an advertisement in the newspapers. They are now divorced.*

One problem with The *Sun*'s argument, however, is that some tabloid stories are not true, and while there may be some justification for exposing the bad behavior of people in positions of respect and authority—such as politicians—ordinary people can also find themselves in the media spotlight.

66 More and more intrusive journalism is prurient and vindictive.... It isn't an attack on the powerful. It is exposure for exposure's sake, directed at anyone whom anyone has ever heard of—and, increasingly, people whom no one has heard of.... If you are the relative of someone who won the lottery or if your dad was famous in the seventies, you're fair game. 99
Andrew Marr, former editor of the Independent newspaper

Diana, Princess of Wales, spent all her adult life in the glare of the media. Editors knew that they could increase circulation simply by putting a photograph of her on their front pages. When she was killed in a car crash in Paris in 1997, while trying to evade photographers, there was a strong public feeling that the media had killed her. There were calls for stronger laws to protect people's privacy but the key problem of balancing the right to privacy with "the right to know" remains.

The issue becomes even more complicated when public figures try to have the best of both worlds, being paid by gossip magazines for photographs of their family wedding, for example, but complaining about media attention on other occasions. Michael Douglas and Catherine Zeta-Jones sued *Hello* magazine for taking unauthorized photographs of their wedding. They won, but the judge said it was not an invasion of privacy.

66 *Those who [bring their private lives to public attention] may place themselves beyond the Press Complaints Commission's protection and must bear the consequences of their actions.* 99 *Lord Wakeham, Chairman, Press Complaints Commission*

▼ Hollywood stars are keen to be in the spotlight when a new movie is launched—but does this mean they have no right to privacy?

▲ The Princess of Wales received both sympathy and criticism for her decision to reveal details of her private life in a TV interview.

Defenders of the tabloids say that readers enjoy such stories, and there is nothing wrong with featuring ordinary people, nor with giving them a chance to "kiss and tell."

66 *It is my experience that it is the small, powerless people who are grateful for the reporter's knock on the door, because it gives them a chance to tell their story.... It is the politicians...who tend to squeal when they come under scrutiny.* 99 *Paul Dacre, editor of the Daily Mail newspaper*

The need to know?

The media are very often criticized for insensitivity and the sensational tone of their reporting. Questions are raised, for example, about the graphic detail provided in crime reports. Sfter the arrests of UK serial killers Fred and Rosemary West, even serious newspapers carried page after page of grisly details about what had been done to the victims. Some people regard this kind of coverage as mere voyeurism, while others argue that it is necessary, in order to make clear the enormity of the crimes.

Similar arguments are used in relation to other news coverage, such as the reporting of wars and natural disasters. Do we always need to be shown the gory details? Should television show pictures of people leaping from the World Trade Center

▲ News reports of atrocities in Bosnia appalled people around the world, but it proved difficult to turn their sense of horror into action.

▼ A Liberian freedom-fighter poses for a picture. Does the need to grab the public's attention get in the way of explaining the issues?

or the dead bodies of Saddam Hussein's two sons?

" Viewers will say…that more suffering is shown than is right and proper, that it is voyeuristic to show such things…some people would prefer not to be told anything about the subject in the first place…. Yet…I didn't feel we were wrong to be there…. The only way to get the West interested in Afghanistan again is to jog the memory of voters across the world. " John Simpson, BBC foreign correspondent

As the BBC's John Simpson points out, the ability of the media to divert people's attention from their everyday affairs to the suffering of others far away is perhaps one of its most important powers. Without news coverage of natural disasters, such as the devastating floods in Sri Lanka and the earthquake in Algeria in 2003, it would be hard to raise money for relief efforts. Hard-hitting reports of atrocities, such as those carried out at the World Trade Center and Pentagon in 2001 and in Bali in 2003, can influence public attitudes and put politicians under intense pressure, either to take action or to change their policies. A famous example was the Vietnam War, which was the first to receive extensive television coverage.

> **Television brought the brutality of war into the comfort of the living room. Vietnam was lost in the living rooms of America—not on the battlefields of Vietnam.**
> *Marshall McLuhan, the Montreal Gazette newspaper*

There is a widely held view that it was the impact of television news that led to the antiwar movement in the USA and to the downfall of President Johnson. However, some people believe that media coverage had a rather different effect.

▼ *News coverage was often critical of Russia during its war with Chechnya. Russian leaders would probably have been happier if the media had stayed at home.*

> **... when seen on a small screen...sometime between the afternoon soapbox drama and the late-night war movie, the television version of the war in Vietnam could appear as just another drama.**
> *Philip Knightly, The First Casualty*

Sensational news reporting can shock us out of apathy and into

▲ *TV coverage of Vietnam helped to turn people against the war. In later conflicts, reporting was much more tightly controlled by the authorities.*

action, but if journalists try to shock us too often, there is a danger that real-life death and violence will become no more important to us than a scene from the movies.

The global village?

It is often said that media technology has made the world smaller. Millions can sit down at the same moment to watch the Olympic Games or the FIFA World Cup soccer final, for example. But what effect does the power of the international media have on people's sense of national identity?

Some people are concerned about the dominance of American programming, claiming that it establishes the American way of life as the one to which everyone should aspire. Research carried out among

▼ *The power of Hollywood movies and glitzy advertising has helped the spread of Western products—even into China.*

Indian children who watch Western television indicates that their viewing does have an impact on their attitudes.

66 *Asked to name the commercials they liked best, many of them mentioned multinational brands such as Coke, Reebok and Nike.... They felt that Indian ads and products were not on a par with Western ones.* 99
Namita Unnikrishnan and Shailaja Bajpai, The Impact of Television Advertising on Children

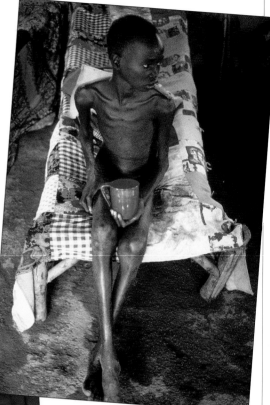

▲*The media alerted the world to the plight of African famine victims, but they are sometimes criticized for focusing only on problems in developing countries.*

However, others believe that such concerns are patronizing toward those involved.

66 *The Indian viewer can protect himself and has enough grounding to know what to reject and what to absorb from foreign programming.* 99 *The Impact of Television Advertising on Children*

◀ The BSE crisis provoked a strongly nationalistic and anti-European response from much of the British press.

There are many occasions when the media have helped to make people aware of the needs and concerns of other communities. In a sense, they make us all part of a "global village."

Unfortunately, there have been other occasions when media coverage has had the opposite effect. In 2003, for example, the USA and Britain became involved in a serious dispute with France over its disapproval of the invasion of Iraq. Coverage of the row in much of the press was strongly nationalistic and anti-French, with many references to their poor fighting spirit in the Second World War.

❝ The Sun goes into battle today over the beef crisis—launching a 'Buy British' crusade aimed at giving Germany a good boot up the Bach-side.… In a showdown rarely seen since the Battle of Britain, the beef fiasco has forced us to fight to save our traditions and freedoms. ❞
The Sun newspaper

Some would argue that such coverage is little more than harmless fun, but other journalists believe it perpetuates prejudices that have no relevance in the world today.

❝ Today we need [Germany's] friendship and sometimes we need its help.… We are pro-German. Yet read much of the press yesterday and you would think Britain loathed the Germans…the British still seem obsessed by Nazism and the war. ❞
The Independent newspaper

Some people see hope for the future. The many channels provided by digital broadcasting could open up the media to a more varied and representative range of views. Online newspapers and magazines could turn readers into active participants.

❝ The…alleged difference is that consumers of cyberspace journalism are not content to be lectured. They will insist on being members of a community of equals. ❞ Michael Kinsley, editor of web magazine Slate

There are question marks over the new technology, as there are over the traditional formats. But there is a possibility that some concerns about the power of the media can be resolved by giving more power back to the individual.

▼ The Internet can open up lines of communication between individuals and powerful public organizations—such as the FBI.

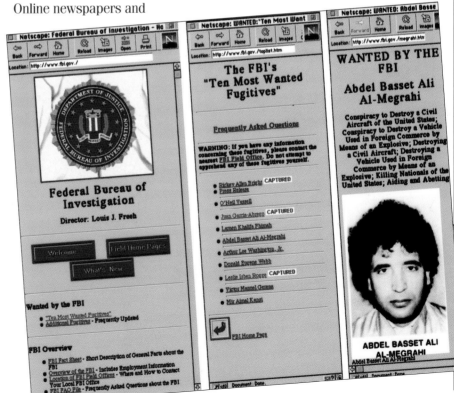

Glossary

AMNESTY INTERNATIONAL: An organization that investigates and protests against human rights abuses.

ANOREXIA (ANOREXIA NERVOSA): A condition that leads a person to diet obsessively.

BIAS: A preference for or prejudice against one group or issue over another.

CENSORSHIP: Banning publication of certain types of material.

CYBERSPACE: An area of virtual reality, such as the inside of a computer system, within which electronic communication occurs.

DEMOCRACY: A system of government in which people vote for representatives to make laws on their behalf.

DIGITAL BROADCASTING: A method of broadcasting that converts sound and picture into codes, like those used by computers. It greatly increases the amount of material that can be transmitted.

DIVERSITY: Difference or variation—a range of varied opinions or objects.

EDITOR: The person in charge of the day-to-day production of a magazine or newspaper.

FASCIST: The word used to describe a government that is very nationalistic, with only a very few people having absolute power.

FBI: The Federal Bureau of Investigation, an organization that investigates crimes.

GRATUITOUS: Something that is done without good reason; unjustified, or motiveless.

HYPOCRISY: Pretending to believe in something or appearing to be virtuous in public, but acting differently in private.

IMPARTIALITY: Fairness; something that is free from prejudice or bias, not favoring one group over another.

INTERNET: The network that transmits information between computers anywhere in the world, via telephones and cable systems.

JUDICIAL: Describes something that is connected to a court of law, or to the administration of justice.

MOGULS: People who have a great deal of power or influence.

PORNOGRAPHIC: Something that is designed to stimulate sexual activity.

PREDISPOSED: A tendency to react in a certain way to a situation or an idea, usually caused by previous emotional or physical experiences.

PROPAGANDA: Information designed to promote support for one group, such as a political party.

PRURIENT: An unhealthy or excessive interest in sexual matters.

SOUNDBITES: Snappy summaries of policies or ideas designed for use during press interviews.

SPIN DOCTOR: A public relations adviser who tries to interpret events—put a "spin" on them—in a way that favors the group he or she represents.

TABLOIDS: Technically, a newspaper printed on small pages, but the word is normally used to describe a newspaper that carries a lot of sex scandals and sensationalized stories.

VOYEURISM: Getting pleasure from seeing or reading about the sex lives of other people, or from scenes of suffering.

Useful addresses

Amnesty International USA
322 8th Ave.
New York, NY 10001;
www.amnesty.org

Fairness and Accuracy in Reporting
(FAIR)
130 W. 25th Street
New York, NY 10001
www.fair.org

Canadian Civil Liberties Association
Suite 200, 394 Bloor Street West
Toronto, ON M5S 1X4
www.ccla.org

The Council of Canadians
502-151 Slater St.
Ottawa, Ontario, K1P 5H3
www.canadians.org

Institute for First Amendment
Studies
P.O. Box 589
Great Barrington, MA 01230
www.ifas.org

National Coalition Against
Censorship
275 Seventh Avenue, 20th Floor,
New York, NY 10001
www.ncac.org

Facts to think about

◆ US teenagers spend nearly $100 billion each year, while teenagers in Europe spend around $40 billion.

◆ Surveys indicate that one in two 11- and 12-year-old girls in the USA are worried about their weight.

◆ British Board of Film Classification figures indicate a downward trend in the number of movies featuring excessive violence. Film distributors can reach a bigger market if movies are classified as suitable for a younger audience.

◆ The Telecommunications Overhaul Bill passed by the U.S. Congress in 1996 allows a single company to own TV stations broadcasting to 35 percent of U.S. households, up from 25 percent.

◆ In the 2000 presidential elections, the Bush campaign spent about $200 million, and the Al Gore campaign spent $120 million. Money spent to win the Florida recount vote was $13.8 million by Bush and $3.2 million by Gore.

◆ During the 2000 presidential elections, the *Washington Post* wrote 75,000 words of biographical information about Al Gore, while the *New York Times* wrote about the same for Bush and Gore combined.

◆ Unlike the USA, Britain has a long traidtion of national newspapers. Those with the biggest sales are the *Sun* and the *Daily Mirror*, with a combined circulation of almost 6 million. The biggest-selling seious papers are the *Daily Telegraph* and *The Times*, totaling around 1.7 million.

◆ The *Daily Mirror* claimed to have increased circulation by around half a million copies when it published revealing photographs of the Duchess of York in 1992.

◆ Access to the Internet is growing at a phenomenal rate. In 2003, there were approximately 655 million users worldwide, with 161 million of these in the USA. These figures do not include cellular phones that also allow Internet access.

◆ The American Medical Association among others has called for a total ban on tobacco advertising. However tobacco companies argue that their ads are aimed at existing smokers and do not encourage nonsmokers to start. They give Norway and Finland as examples of countries where smoking continued to increase after tobacco advertising was banned.

Index